JN 0315192S

FAMOUS PEOPLE
FAMOUS LIVES

Biographies of famous people to
support the curriculum.

Emmeline Pankhurst

by Emma Fischel

Illustrations by Martin Remphry

W
FRANKLIN WATTS
LONDON•SYDNEY

First published in 2000 by J B PAN
Franklin Watts
96 Leonard Street
London
EC2A 4XD

Franklin Watts Australia
14 Mars Road
Lane Cove
NSW 2066

ISBN: 0 7496 3675 0

Dewey Decimal Classification Number: 324.6

A CIP catalogue record for this book
is available from the British Library.

Series editor: Sarah Ridley
Historical consultant: Barbara Searle

Printed in Great Britain

Emmeline Pankhurst

When Emmeline was born, a lot of people thought being a girl wasn't as good as being a boy.

"Boys should learn important things," they said. "But girls don't need to. Men are in charge of everything!"

But Emmeline grew up wanting to change all that.

Emmeline had a happy childhood. Her parents were kind and rich, and they tried to help others who weren't so lucky.

Sometimes Emmeline helped too.

HELP
THE POOR
AND NEEDY.

DONATIONS
PLEASE!

But she soon learned what lay
ahead in life, even for rich girls.

Her five younger brothers
could grow up to be doctors,
or lawyers or do exciting things.

She and her four younger
sisters were expected to sit at
home and wait for a husband.

When Emmeline was 14 she went
to a meeting with her mother.
It was all about something called
'the vote'.

People who voted could choose
who would lead the country and
make the laws. Men could vote
but women couldn't.

Emmeline listened hard at
the meeting.

"The laws and rules are made
by men and unfair to women!"
said the speaker. "Women must
have the vote and help make
new laws!"

Emmeline's parents gave her more education than most girls – but only because Emmeline insisted on it.

There weren't many schools for older girls then. Emmeline went to one in France.

But when she came home
she didn't know what to do
next. Then she met Richard
Marsden Pankhurst ...

and married him when she was
just 21. He was 40.

Richard was a fine lawyer but he didn't earn much money. He spent most of his time helping people who couldn't afford to pay.

"Be a politician," Emmeline said. "Then you could change things."

But back then a lot of people found his ideas shocking and they didn't vote for him.

Emmeline and her father had a huge quarrel about Richard. They never spoke again.

He's becoming a crank and he's making you one too!

By now Emmeline and Richard
had four children – and a plan.
"We'll move to London and
I'll open a shop," she said.
"We'll make lots of money."

But no one in that part of London
wanted to buy the sort of things
her shop sold.

Then Frank, their son, became very ill. In the end he died.

"Dirty streets, bad drains – you're lucky it's just one child dead!" said the doctor. "It's always the poor who die young!"

One bitter winter they moved back to Manchester. Emmeline soon saw how terrible life was for the very poor. Many lived in workhouses. They were filthy, horrible places.

These people need good food, warm clothes, clean bedding and chairs for the old. And that's just the start ...

Some people preferred to starve rather than go there. The politicians did nothing to help, so the Pankhursts did.

"The rich have so much," said Emmeline. "And the poor almost nothing. If only women had the power to change things!"

When Emmeline was 30 she visited her old schoolfriend in France. News came that Richard was ill, so she raced home.

She was too late – he was dead.

Now Emmeline needed to work to feed her family. In her new job she found out even more about how hard life was for the poor.

"I can change nothing without a voice and a vote," said Emmeline. And she knew then what she had to do ...

Emmeline formed an organisation, helped by her daughter, Christabel.

She spoke on street corners, in parks ... anywhere she could.

There were three main groups of politicians. Emmeline needed to get them to change the law.

"I'll help," said Keir Hardie, the Labour leader.

But the Conservatives made sure he failed.

There was one more group to try.

"Will you Liberals give us the vote?" Christabel asked. But they wouldn't even speak to her.

So she tried to make them answer – and SHE made front page news.

Three days later she was freed. That evening's meeting was the biggest yet!

"We must be noticed!" said
Emmeline to her followers.
"Shout! Interrupt! Be a nuisance!"

"Shout? Interrupt? We can't
do THAT!" said lots of them.
"We don't know how."

So Emmeline showed them.

Before long, no politician was safe ... however important.

But soon the police learned
to spot the women.

"They throw us out before
we can speak," said Emmeline.
"So hide your banners and
flags. Hide your faces. Let no
one suspect you. THEN attack!"

"This is no way for women
to behave," thundered the
politicians.

"It is the only way," said
Emmeline. "We WILL
make people know about us!"
And she carried on planning,
day and night.

"Now for our first march!" said Emmeline. "To the Houses of Parliament."

Four hundred women joined her. But the doors were barred when they got there.

"They may bar us," said Emmeline. "But they won't stop us. The fight goes on!"

And so the demonstrations got bigger and bigger.

Now Emmeline was 50 and busier than ever. "I need help to get everything done," she said.

"I know just the people," said Keir Hardie. "They're important, they're clever and they're good at raising money!"

Emmeline, please meet Frederick and Emmeline Pethick-Lawrence.

W.S.P.U. NEW MEMBERS

TO: EMMELINE PANKHURST

TO E. PANKHURST

Times were changing. Women were becoming doctors and they were going to universities – but still politicians did nothing about the vote. Women were running out of patience.

BROKEN PROMISES

1870
1884
1905
1906

EMMELINE PANKHURST
LABOUR PARTY
MEMBERSHIP CARD

More and more women joined
Emmeline every day.

"Tell us what to do," they
begged her. "You make us feel
strong and proud and brave!"

The women shouted louder and louder. The police got rougher and rougher.

And then two women smashed the windows of the Prime Minister's house with stones. A new way of fighting had begun.

"Stop!" said some women to Emmeline. "Shouting and fighting is not ladylike. It will make men *less* likely to give us the vote."

"Stop!" said others. "Women shouldn't try to be clever. Men can tell us what to think!"

Emmeline was jeered at and spat at – and, one time, even kicked to the ground.

Over the years she had very little money. She lost her job. She lost friends. And time and again she was put in prison.

33

And still nothing changed.
"The Prime Minister is not
doing enough," said Emmeline.
"He is not doing ANYTHING.
We must march once again."

Emmeline and 450 women marched to Parliament but the Prime Minister wouldn't see any of them. What happened next became known as Black Friday.

"We will NOT give up!" said Emmeline.

The politicians got fed up.
Even the King got fed up.
But they still did nothing.

"Smash all their windows!" said Emmeline. "We women are angry, so show it!"

And one day in March they went to the busiest shopping street in London and showed just how angry they were ...

Huge crowds of women were in prison now. Emmeline was often one of them – but even prison didn't stop her.

"Make trouble!" she said. "Shout! Scream! Break things!"

And the women did.

"We will suffer anything," they said. "We will lose our jobs, our homes, our freedom. We will follow Mrs Pankhurst to death if need be!"

"There's too much violence,"
said some.

"There's not enough!" said
Emmeline. "We must do more!
For fifty years women worked
peacefully for the vote. For fifty
years they did not get it!"

Then there was a terrible accident.

A woman called Emily Davison tried to stop a big horse race to protest about having no vote. But one of the horses knocked her down and killed her.

Emmeline was 55 now and back in prison.

"Give us the vote or give us death!" she said, then she refused to eat. So did most of the other women in prison.

"Force-feed them," ordered the King. It was a horrible, painful thing.

They tried to force-feed
Emmeline too – but she wouldn't
let them.

So each time she was near death
they let her go, then when she
was well again they put her back
in prison.

CAT AND MOUSE ACT
1913

FREE THEM WHEN WEAK
AND NEAR DEATH.
PUT THEM BACK IN PRISON
WHEN BETTER.

She almost died.

The next year the First World War broke out. "Help us!" said the politicians, freeing her and all the other women in prison. "People listen to you."

"Votes must wait," said Emmeline. "There is a war to be won!"

"Splendid work by you women," said the politicians once the war was won. And they gave the vote to women over 30.

Ten years later the vote was given to all women over 21 and Emmeline's struggle was over.

Only a few weeks later, she died.

Further facts

Suffragettes

Emmeline and her followers
were known as suffragettes.
The name came from the word
suffrage, which means being allowed
to vote. Today, all men and women
can vote at the age of 18.

Votes for women

Emmeline never
stopped thinking
of new ways to
get publicity.
Suffragettes
dropped leaflets
from hot air balloons.
They went up and down

rivers on boats, shouting through megaphones. They chalked on pavements. They walked around wearing sandwich boards. They even brought out a board game with dice, a bit like *Snakes and Ladders*. It was called *Suffragettes In and Out of Prison*!

Stone collecting and throwing

The suffragettes threw stones in their protests, to break windows. As it wasn't easy to find stones in London, some of the women drove into the countryside at night to collect them. Emmeline herself was not a good shot, and despite practice, she didn't manage to break any windows on the Downing Street raid.

Some important dates in Emmeline Pankhurst's lifetime

1858 Emmeline Goulden is born.

1879 Emmeline marries Richard Pankhurst.

1880 Emmeline's daughter, Christabel, is born.

1898 Richard Pankhurst dies.

1903 The Women's Social and Political Union (WSPU) is formed.

1906 The first march to the Houses of Parliament. Emmeline goes to prison for the first time.

1909 The first suffragette goes on hunger strike.

1910 The police are very rough with protesters on Black Friday.

1912 Women storm the West End of London with axes and hammers.

1913 Emily Davison dies. Emmeline spends a year in and out of prison.

1914 World War I begins.

1918 World War I ends. Women over 30 are given the vote.

1928 Women over 21 are given the vote. Emmeline dies.